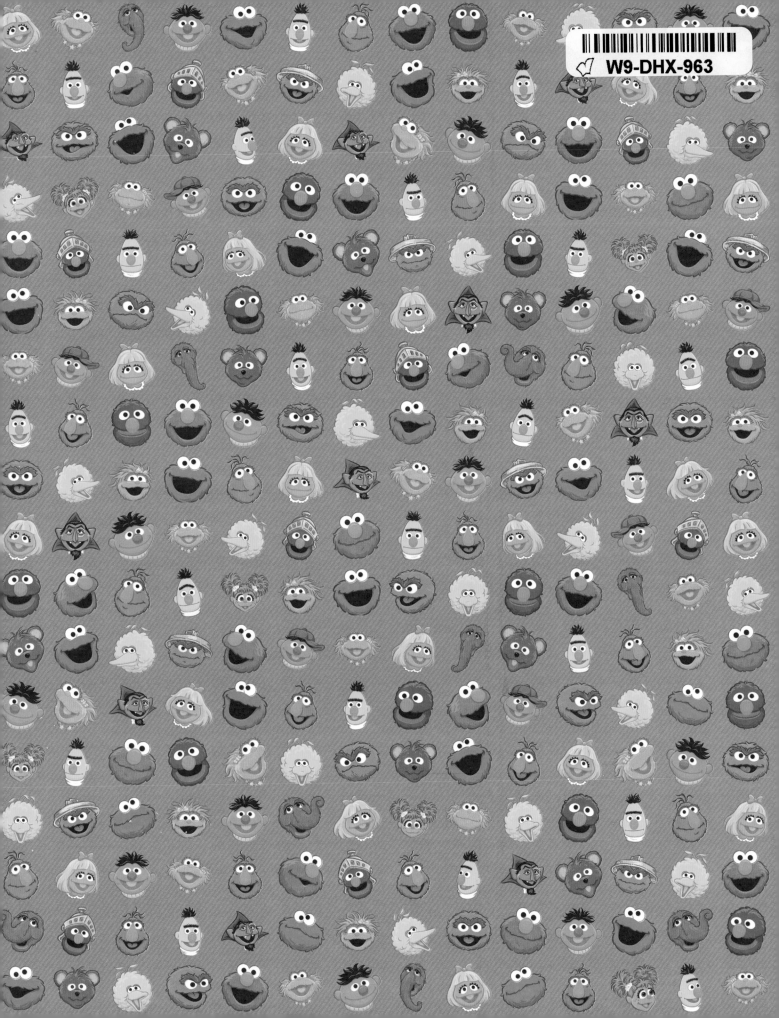

First published by Parragon in 2009

Parragon
Queen Street House
4 Queen Street
Bath BA1 1HE, UK

ISBN 978-1-4075-7197-3

Printed in China

123 SESAME STREET®

Nature Crafts

PaRragon

Bath · New York · Singapore · Hong Kong · Cologne · Delhi · Melbourne

TIPS FOR SUCCESS

Prepare your space

Cover your workspace with newspaper or a plastic or paper tablecloth. Make sure you and your children are wearing clothes (including shoes!) that you don't mind becoming spattered with food, paint, or glue. But relax! You'll never completely avoid mess; in fact, it's part of the fun!

Wash your hands

Wash your hands (and your child's hands) before starting a new project, and clean up as you go along. Clean hands make for clean crafts! Remember to wash your hands afterward, too, using soap and warm water to get off any of the remaining materials.

Follow steps carefully

Follow each step carefully, and in the sequence in which it appears. We've tested all the projects; we know they work, and we want them to work for you, too. Also, ask your children, if they are old enough, to read along with you as you work through the steps. For a younger child, you can direct her to look at the pictures on the page to try to guess what the next step is.

Measure precisely

If a project gives you measurements, use your ruler, T-square, measuring cups, or measuring spoons to make sure you measure as accurately as you can. Sometimes the success of the project may depend on it. Also, this is a great opportunity to teach measuring techniques to your child.

Be patient

You may need to wait while something bakes or leave paint, glue, or clay to dry, sometimes for a few hours or even overnight. Encourage your child to be patient as well; explain to her why she must wait, and, if possible, find ways to entertain her as you are waiting. For example you can show her how long you have to wait by pointing out the time on a clock.

Clean up

When you've finished your project, clean up any mess. Store all the materials together so that they are ready for the next time you want to craft. Ask your child to help.

BIRD BATH

YOU WILL NEED

- Colored oven-bake clay
- Rolling pin and knife
- Metal or plastic plate with wide flat rim
- Plastic gloves
- Spatula
- Grout
- Old cloth
- Varnish
- Paintbrush

1 Roll out the clay thinly. Cut out enough square tiles to cover the plate rim. Harden the tiles in the oven following the manufacturer's instructions.

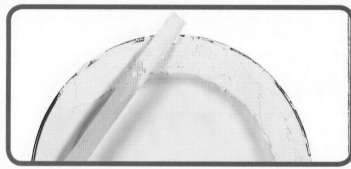

2 Put on the plastic gloves and use the spatula to spread a layer of tile grout across the rim of the plate.

3

KIDS

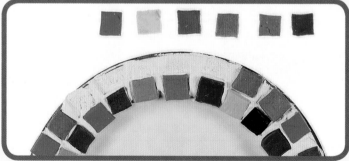

Press the tiles into the grout, working round the rim of the plate. Leave a narrow space between each tile. Leave to set for 24 hours.

④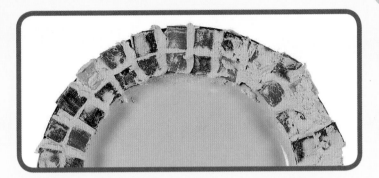

Use the spatula to carefully fill in between the tiles with more grout. Allow to dry for 24 hours.

⑤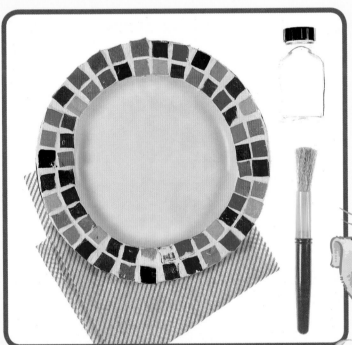

Wipe off all of the extra grout, then polish up the tiles with a cloth. Now apply a layer of varnish with a paintbrush to give them a shine.

DID YOU KNOW?
All birds have wings but not all birds can fly!

Try using craft jewels to decorate your plate.

BIRD FEEDER

YOU WILL NEED

- Empty milk or juice carton
- Scissors
- Paint and paintbrush
- Strong tape
- String
- Birdseed

①

Cut away the four sides of the milk or juice carton, leaving space at the base to hold the birdseed.

 2 KIDS

Paint your bird feeder inside and out. You may want to choose a color that will blend in with the surroundings, such as green or brown.

③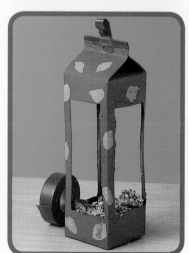

Decorate your bird feeder. Then attach a piece of strong tape in a loop to the top of the feeder and fill the base with some birdseed.

4 Hang up your bird feeder with string in a place safely out of the reach of cats.

DID YOU KNOW? It's hard for birds to find food in winter. You can help by making bird feeders and keeping them filled.

Thread some peanuts on string and hang it up by the feeder. Birds will love it!

FLOWER CROWN

YOU WILL NEED

- 10 pipe cleaners
- Tissue paper (different colors)
- Scissors
- White glue and brush
- Pencil
- Craft gems

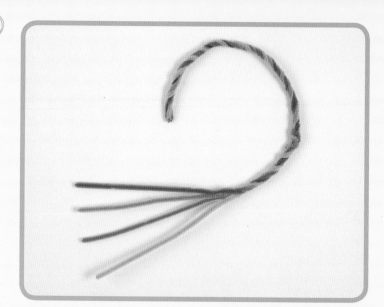

1

Twist four pipe cleaners together to make half the headband. Repeat this with four more, then twist the ends together to make the whole headband.

2

KIDS

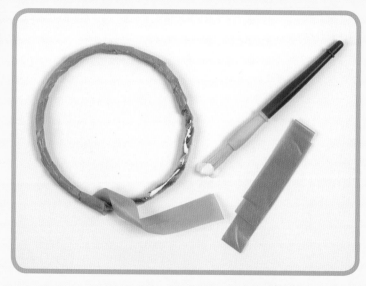

Brush glue over the headband. Wrap one inch-wide strips of green tissue paper around it, to cover it entirely.

③

Draw and cut out 42 tissue paper flower shapes. Snip the last two pipe cleaners into pieces 2 inches long. Layer six tissue flowers together then push a bent piece of pipe cleaner in then out of the middle, so both ends stick out.

④

Twist the ends of the pipe cleaners around the hoop to attach the flowers to the headband. Trim off the ends of the pipe cleaner. Carefully scrunch the petals, and glue craft gems in the middle of each flower.

DID YOU KNOW? Long, long ago, people wore wreaths in their hair to show they were royalty.

BOTTLE GARDENS

YOU WILL NEED

- Sticks
- Old spoon
- Wire
- Kitchen sponge
- Cottonball
- Large jar with lid
- Pebbles or gravel
- Suitable potting compost
- Suitable plants, such as ivy and vine
- Paint
- Awl or screwdriver

①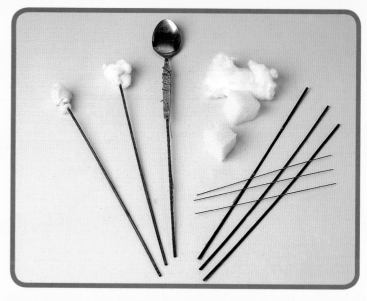

Use an old spoon attached with wire to a long stick for a digging tool. Use sponge wired onto a stick to press the earth down when planting. For a cleaning tool, use a cottonball wired onto a stick.

 2 KIDS

Pour a thin layer of pebbles or gravel in the base of the bottle. Now cover the pebbles with a thick layer of potting compost. Press the compost down with your sponge tool.

③

Use the digging tool to place individual plants in position. Press the compost down firmly around the plants. Use the cottonball tool to clean up the sides of the bottle garden.

④

Carefully make holes in the lid using the awl or screwdriver. Use paint to decorate the bottle garden with any pattern you like. Put the lid on and place your garden in a place with lots of daylight, but not in direct sunlight.

DID YOU KNOW?
Plant roots grow lots of tiny hairs near their tip to "drink" in water from the soil.

Choose low-growing plants, and water your bottle garden every two weeks in the summer.

PLANT POTS

YOU WILL NEED

- Old gardening pots, margarine or yogurt tubs, kitchen containers
- Acrylic paint in different colors
- Paintbrushes

1
KIDS

Make sure the pots are clean and dry. Paint on a base coat, then cover the pot completely. You may need to do several coats of paint to cover it well. Let dry.

2
KIDS

Paint any pattern you like on the pot. It's fun to paint on things such as borders, flowers, or animals. Practice drawing some ideas on paper before painting them on the pot.

3
KIDS

To make smaller plant pots, paint your yogurt cartons in lots of bright colors. They make perfect containers for smaller, or young plants or herbs.

DID YOU KNOW? Green plants use energy from light to grow and stay a healthy green color.

To keep from making a mess, Elmo covers the work area with newspapers before beginning.

LEAF PICTURES

YOU WILL NEED

- Fall leaves (different shapes and sizes)
- Heavy book (e.g. dictionary)
- White glue
- Picture frame
- Paintbrush
- Acrylic paints: black, gold
- Sponge
- Saucer

1 KIDS

Choose some leaves with interesting shapes and colors. Place them between the pages of a heavy book. Leave them for several weeks to flatten and dry.

2 KIDS

Arrange the dry leaves on a sheet of paper. Glue them down and ask an adult to put the paper in a frame.

Elmo makes leaf people. A leaf could be a body or a head. Then draw the rest of the picture around it.

3 KIDS

To make an even more decorative picture, paint the leaves black. When dry, sponge on gold paint in patches and leave to dry.

MINI BUG POTS

YOU WILL NEED

- Air-drying clay
- Water
- Acrylic paints
- Paintbrushes
- White glue and brush
- Water-based varnish

1

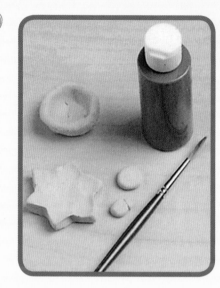

Push your thumbs into a ball of clay to make the pot shape, smoothing it with your fingers. Make a lid out of a flat disk of clay. Stretch it into a flower shape, then make a ladybug from a ball of clay.

2

KIDS

Paint the pot, lid and ladybug, allowing them to dry between colors. When completely dry, glue the bug to the lid. Apply a coat of varnish over the whole thing.

Experiment with different shaped pots and creepy crawlies. Let your imagination go!

DID YOU KNOW? There are more kinds of insects in the world than any other type of creature.

Oh, what a cute little bug!

DRIED FLOWERS

YOU WILL NEED

- Florist's foam
- Knife
- Ceramic pot
- A selection of dried flowers
- White glue and brush
- Scissors
- Ribbon
- Acrylic paints

①

Cut the florist's foam with the knife and fit it into the flowerpot. Ask a grown-up to help you do this.

② KIDS

Press bunches of dried flowers into the foam, around the edge of the flower pot. Try to keep them all at the same height.

3
KIDS

Glue dried moss around the edge of the pot. Using scissors, trim the moss all the way around, so it is even.

④

Use a little glue to stick some dried flowers in the center to finish off your design. Trim off any untidy bits with a pair of scissors.

DID YOU KNOW?
Plants make oil in their leaves to stop them drying out in strong sunshine.

Tie ribbon around your pot or paint it with colorful patterns to make it look extra special.

SEASHELL MOBILES

YOU WILL NEED

- Seashells
- String
- Scissors
- Paintbrush
- Varnish
- Driftwood or branch

①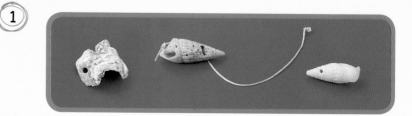

Thread the string through the first shell and tie a large knot underneath, to hold the shell in place. Find shells that already have holes in them, so you won't have to make them.

②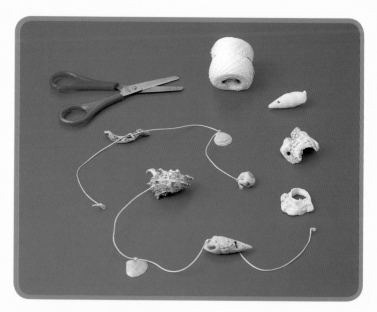

Continue threading on shells, tying a knot each time. Make as many separate shell strings as you like.

③ KIDS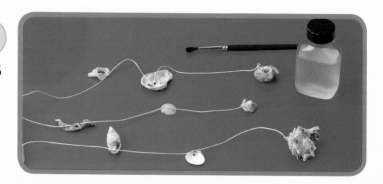

Varnish the shells and leave to dry.

④

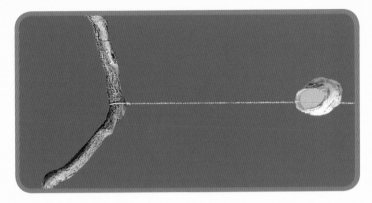

Make loops at the end of the shell strings to hang them from a piece of driftwood or a branch. Check the mobile for balance as you put them on.

⑤

KIDS

Hang up your pretty seashell mobile where you can see it, to remind you of a happy vacation.

PRESSED FLOWERS

YOU WILL NEED

- Fresh flowers
- Flower press or heavy book (e.g. dictionary)
- Scissors
- White glue and brush
- Items to decorate, such as ready-made cards or boxes

1 KIDS

Press the flowers flat in a flower press or inside a heavy book. Keep the flowers in place for about three weeks before you use them. Dried flowers crumble easily so handle them carefully.

2 KIDS

Use them to make greeting cards. You can buy prepared cards to decorate or make your own from good quality paper. Use a little glue to attach the pressed flowers to the card. Paint on a little varnish to give the picture a glossy finish.

③

Make a flower picture. Press a whole flower in your flower press, or book. When ready, stick it on the card. Choose a small frame and place the pressed flower in it.

④

If you press lots of flowers you may have enough to cover a small box. Varnish it.

DID YOU KNOW? Bees like blue or violet blue flowers best. Most birds like red flowers best of all.

Make sure that your flowers have no insects in them. And especially, make sure you have permission to pick the flowers.

DESERT GARDENS

YOU WILL NEED

- Flowerpot
- Gravel
- Old spoon or small garden trowel
- Cactus potting compost
- Cactus plants
- Suitable gloves
- Selection of stones
- White sand

1 KIDS

Place a layer of gravel in the flowerpot. This will provide drainage for your plants.

2 KIDS

Add a layer of cactus potting compost and press it down firmly.

3

Put on your gloves, then dig small holes in the compost and plant the cacti.

4
KIDS

DID YOU KNOW?
Deserts get very little rain. Only special plants and animals can survive there.

Me like painting lizards, snakes, and desert animals on pots.

Cover the compost with a layer of white sand. This will make it look like desert sand. Add stones to make it look like a desert scene. Place your pot by a window and water the plants when the soil gets dry.

FLOWER POTS

YOU WILL NEED

- Spatula
- Grout
- Ceramic plant pot or container
- Seashells
- White glue and brush
- Varnish
- Acrylic paints (optional)
- Paintbrush

1 KIDS

Use a spatula to apply a thick layer of grout along the rim of the pot.

2 KIDS

Press the seashells firmly into the grout. Leave the grout to dry.

3 KIDS

When dry, varnish the shells to bring out their natural colors.

4

KIDS

For a different look, paint your pot.

DID YOU KNOW?
Shells are homes to mollusks, which are animals with soft bodies and no bones.

5

KIDS

When the paint is dry, use strong glue to attach some shells.

6

KIDS

When dry, varnish the shells. Leave to dry again, then put a plant in your pot.

ANIMAL CLIPS

YOU WILL NEED

- Thin cardboard
- Pencil
- Scissors
- Marker pens: red, yellow
- Eraser
- White glue and brush
- Clothespins

1 KIDS

Carefully draw the outline of an animal's head on the cardboard with a pencil.

2 KIDS

When you are happy with your animal design, color it in using colored markers.

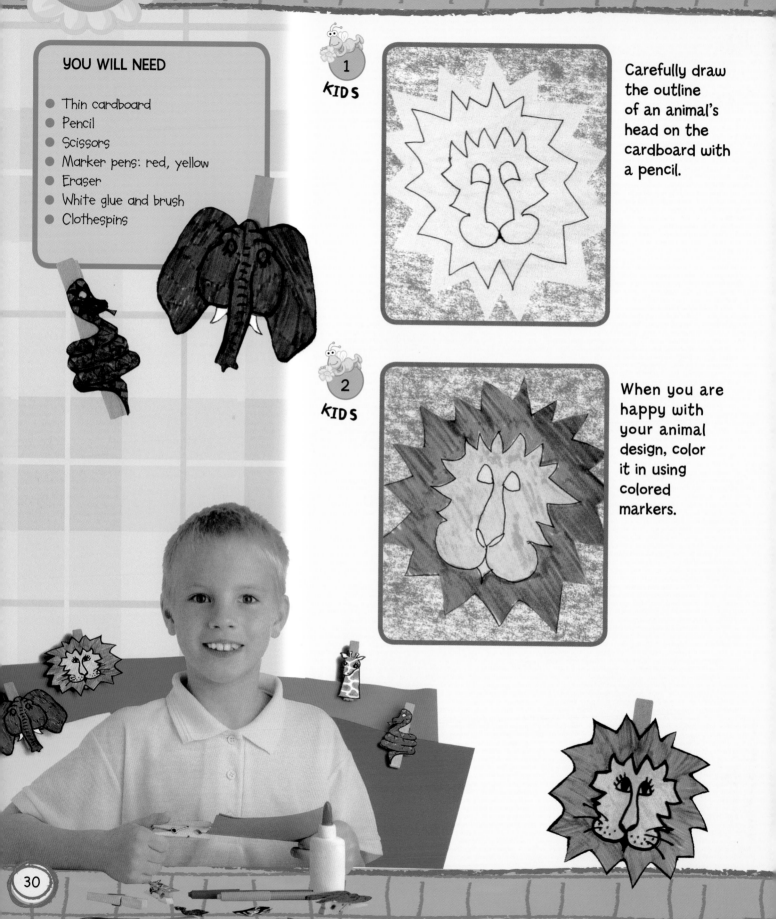

3
KIDS

Then draw a dark outline around the colored animal. Cut out your animal and glue it onto a clothespin. Now it is ready to hold your notes!

DID YOU KNOW? An adult lion's roar can be heard up to five miles away. ROARRR!

If you want, glue the clip onto a magnet and put it on the fridge.

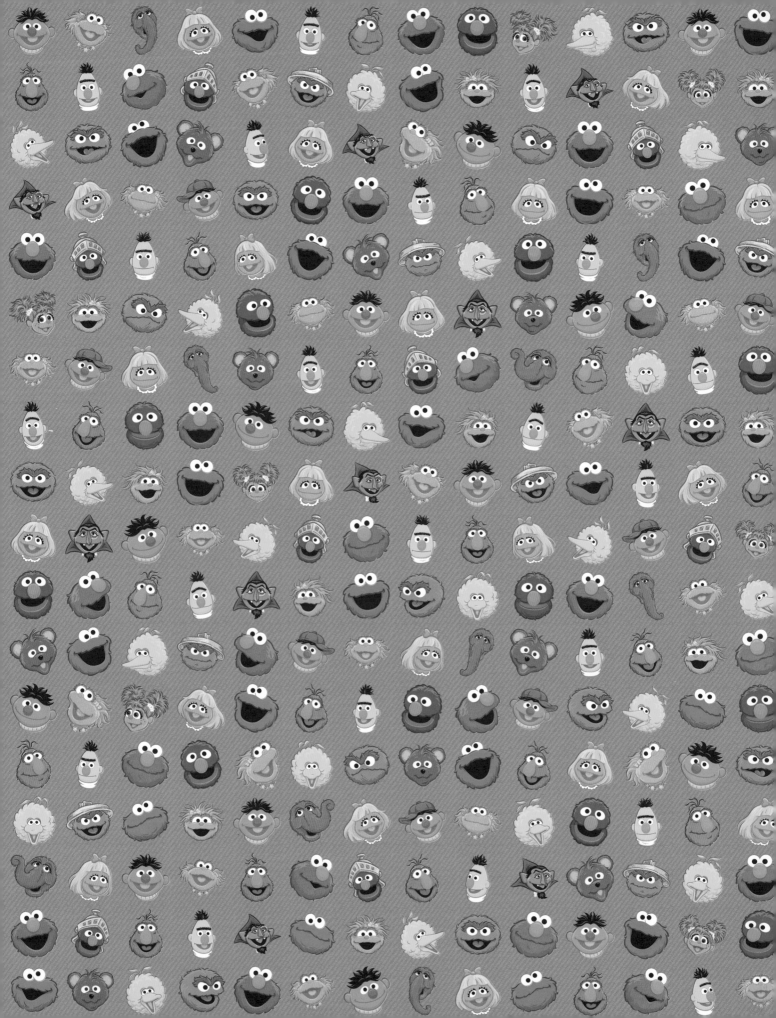